LIVING AND LOVED

Dear God, who through the fabric of this place,
Its strong oak timbers and soothing stone
The consecrated altar beauty and the windows' vivid panes,
Knew of praise and joy and longing in the minds
Of generations kneeling quietly here,
Please hear us, in our turn
And know our thankfulness
For confidence in your peace, eternity.
Aware too, after last Blessing by Christ's priest,
When the heavy doors swing open to the mundane street,
That we have left a little gift of ourselves
To strengthen this, your sanctuary of peace.

ERIC GLADWIN

$\mathcal{L}$IVING & $\mathcal{L}$OVED
─ A CELEBRATION OF CHURCHES ─

PAM RHODES

PHOTOGRAPHS BY JOHN ROGERS

A LION BOOK

Copyright © 2000 Pam Rhodes
Photographs copyright © 2000 John Rogers
This edition copyright © 2000 Lion Publishing

The author asserts the moral right
to be identified as the author of this work

Published by
Lion Publishing plc
Sandy Lane West, Oxford, England
www.lion-publishing.co.uk
ISBN 0 7459 4289 X

First edition 2000
10 9 8 7 6 5 4 3 2 1 0

Text Acknowledgments
'Dear God, who through the fabric of this place...'
by Eric Gladwin. Reproduced by permission of the author

Picture Acknowledgments
Maps of Caernarvonshire, Cambridgeshire,
Derbyshire, Staffordshire, Lancashire, Kent,
Rutland Shire and Anglesea supplied by Mary
Evans Picture Library and reproduced
by permission

Map of Han Shire (Gough Maps Berkshire 6)
reproduced courtesy of the Bodleian Library, Oxford

A catalogue record for this book is available
from the British Library

Typeset in 9.75/18 Modern 880
Printed and bound in Indonesia

Contents

Preface

One of the treasures of this country is its churches, and Pam Rhodes has had the privilege of visiting many of them over the years. But Pam never goes merely as a visitor. Rather she goes as a pilgrim, ready to meet with the God and Father of our Lord Jesus Christ, who has been worshipped in that building for decades, or even centuries, and whom the living congregation of Christians still worship today.

In LIVING AND LOVED *Pam has captured that sense of being a pilgrim, enjoying every evidence of a vibrant active faith. It is a book which I am sure many who love church buildings and, more importantly, love our Lord, will greatly enjoy and I warmly commend it to you.*

GEORGE CAREY,
ARCHBISHOP OF CANTERBURY

Introduction

I love churches. I spend a lot of time in them. Over thirteen years of presenting BBC Television's *Songs of Praise*, I've sung along with local congregations in churches of every size and history the length and breadth of Great Britain. I've celebrated Easter in great cathedrals, Harvest in tiny villages and Christmas in beautifully decorated town churches. I've visited hospice chapels, modern buildings resounding to the rhythm of rock bands, and ancient sites where worship has taken place far back into the mists of time. And wherever I've been, however grand or basic the church, I've always found God there.

Some people love sacred buildings because of the architecture. Some are fascinated by their history. For me, the heart of a church is its people – those who raised the money to build it, the craftsmen who had the inspiration and skill to design it, and the congregations whose devotion and personality have shaped it over the years. This book is a celebration of that Christian spirit. It is PC – and by that I mean *personal choice*, not 'politically correct'. The geographical spread is not as fair as it could be; the denominations are not represented in perfect proportion –

but what you have here is a selection of churches and chapels that have inspired and moved me, and which I think you will appreciate too.

I have asked other friends to help me with the choice of churches to be included. The Archbishops of Canterbury and York, James Galway, Terry Waite, Dame Cicely Saunders, Patrick Lichfield and Barbara Erskine are among those who have shared their favourite places and thoughts. Their contribution has added depth, knowledge and perception for which I am really grateful.

Most of all, my thanks go to my very dear friend John Rogers, who is simply a superb photographer. Over the years that I've known him, his ability to tell a story in a single shot has brought him great admiration and recognition. He is one of Britain's leading magazine photographers, mostly known for his candid pictures of show-business personalities in films and television dramas. For me, his immediate enthusiasm for the challenge of capturing the spirit and personality of church buildings was an inspiration. John's photographs reveal the essence of these places of worship which are truly LIVING AND LOVED.

St Hywyn's Church
ABERDARON, WALES

Back in the mists of time, many a pilgrim made their way down to the very tip of the Llyn Peninsula in the north-west corner of Wales, to gaze from the shore at Aberdaron, across Cardigan Bay towards Bardsey, 'the isle of 20,000 saints'. Today, the pilgrims may arrive by car, and the delightful teashops of this little fishing village may tempt them with comforting mugs of frothy coffee and butter-laden teacakes to help them on their way – but the effect, as they stand on this windswept, unspoilt headland, is much the same as ever. There has been a church on this spot for around 1,500 years, and St Hywyn's Church, named after a little-known abbot of Bardsey, has become known as the Cathedral of Llyn, the last resting place for pilgrims on their way to St Mary's Abbey over on the island.

The church stands precariously perched above the beach on a high defence wall designed to protect it from the battering sea. In fact, St Hywyn's was almost abandoned in the 1840s when years of erosion and disrepair threatened to make a ruin of the building. A brand new edifice was constructed at the top of the hill, but all was not well. Some say it was just that folk in this corner of Wales have a particular affection for revered old buildings. Others think that God simply refused to move house up the hill. Whatever the reason, the church on the hill ended up as a mortuary, while the pews of St Hywyn's filled again.

It was probably because of the large number of pilgrims who visited over the years that, towards the end of the fifteenth century, the original Norman building was doubled in size, creating two naves separated from each other by lofty columns. At that time, much of the church floor was probably made available to the pilgrims to sleep on,

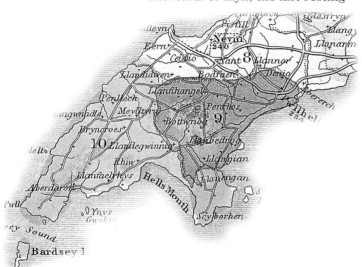

with a screen across the altar area to keep it sacred.

For such an ancient church, St Hywyn's is surprisingly light and airy inside, with sunlight streaming through the plain-glass windows. Ministers who serve there speak of the inspiration of being able to glimpse the wild beauty of the sea beyond as they stand at the altar. With its medieval arches, octagonal pillars and roof timbers, centuries of devotion are etched into the very fabric of this cherished place of worship. One such worshipper was Reverend R.S. Thomas, well known in Wales as a poet, remembered with affection locally for his years of

■ ST HYWYN'S CHURCH,
Aberdaron, Wales

ministry at St Hywyn's. It was he who donated the corona of candles that catch the eye above the beautifully ornate pulpit.

Standing in the centre of what was once a completely round graveyard, characteristic of this part of Wales, St Hywyn's has a timeless air of holiness. If you only manage to visit one church in this book, make it this one.

I shall never forget my first sight of Ampleforth Abbey. I had driven northwards from York, finally cutting across the bottom of the farmland that stretches out below the magnificent spread of monastery and school. In spite of a light covering of snow, which lent an eerie glare to the strangely silent landscape, the honey-coloured buildings with their elegant grey roofs were warmly welcoming, drawing attention to what is both visually and spiritually the heart of Ampleforth: its abbey church. Its dominant position on the skyline is a symbol of God unifying every aspect of both individual and community life. Whether a monk, schoolboy or visitor, you feel a powerful sense of God drawing together thought, work and worship within these walls, reaching out to all who come into contact with the Ampleforth community.

Following a way of life that was set out by St Benedict nearly 1,500 years ago, there are now about 100 Ampleforth monks, with just over half based at the monastery, and the

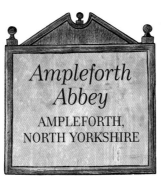

Ampleforth Abbey

AMPLEFORTH,
NORTH YORKSHIRE

others dispersed in small monasteries and parishes in Lancashire, York, Cumbria, and even further afield, like Zimbabwe. Ampleforth's work has always been apostolic – to bring others closer to God – and for that reason the school was founded 200 years ago when a group of monks from Dieulouard in Lorraine first established a small community here. Today, the 500 boys at the school worship in the abbey church at least once a week, while the monks gather there five or six times a day for Mass and Sung Office. A traditional part of their worship is plainsong, for which the monks are well known. This haunting repetitious chanting, together with the Latin wording for the Mass, both of which have provided atmosphere and focus for worship around the world for centuries, adds a timeless quality to the services at Ampleforth Abbey.

Mostly the monks share Mass in the intimacy of the choir, which is divided from the rest of the church by the ornate high altar crowned with

*FACING PAGE:
At prayer in
the crypt*

*BELOW:
Procession of
monks into
morning
mass*

the image of the crucified Christ.
Sir Giles Gilbert Scott, who was also
the architect of the huge Anglican
cathedral in Liverpool, designed this
part of the abbey first, in the 1920s.
Later he completed the rest, creating
a light, airy feel for this simple cross-
shaped area with its pale stone walls,
tall pillars and graceful arches.

To one side of the choir stands
the Holy Souls' memorial chapel
commemorating pupils of the school
who gave their lives in the First World
War – and the sturdy, weather-worn
altar stone in St Benet's Chapel was
brought here from the nearby ruin
of Byland Abbey, which in medieval
times had the largest monastery nave
in Europe.

The crypt is unusual in that it is not
underneath the abbey church, but at
ground level, with a collection of
twenty-five small chapels in which
monks can find solitude and peace for
private prayer. There was a time when
monks were duty-bound to say Mass
each at a separate altar, before the
Vatican Council brought in liturgical
changes some thirty years ago, which
allowed Mass to be celebrated jointly.

However, for many in this busy monastic community, the opportunity to pray alone is still personally fulfilling, and often throughout the day you may come across a brother in one of these chapels kneeling in prayer.

The abbot who oversaw those changes from Rome during the 1960s was Basil Hume, who went on to become the much-loved Cardinal Archbishop of Westminster in 1976. Since his death in 1999, many have spoken of the holiness of the man who often described himself as a

■ AMPLEFORTH ABBEY,
Ampleforth,
North Yorkshire

monk at heart. It was probably here
in these small crypt chapels that Basil
felt most at home – a simple man of
faith, alone in prayer, but very much
a part of the loving, encompassing
whole of the Ampleforth community.

RIGHT:
Monks gathering in
the cloisters

14

ABOVE:
Statue of St Benedict

St Aidan's Church
BAMBURGH, NORTHUMBERLAND

Once visited, never forgotten – that's Bamburgh. Nestling around its fairy-tale castle, what was once a bustling town is now a quiet Northumberland village. Alongside it rages the North Sea, iron grey as it stretches away to the Farne Islands, and to Lindisfarne, known as Holy Island since St Aidan chose it as his Episcopal seat when he made his way south from Iona in 635. He was invited by Oswald, King of Northumbria and resident of Bamburgh Castle, and through the shared faith and friendship of these two men Christianity was established as a strong presence throughout the North of England.

When St Aidan was taken ill in Bamburgh in 651, it's said that he laid his head on a wooden beam which has since survived two devastating fires unscathed. Three churches have stood on the spot where St Aidan died, and in the present parish church, which was built around the start of the thirteenth century, that wooden beam is now suspended above the font, a poignant link between the saint and the church named after him.

St Aidan's Church is an imposing sight as it stands on the headland in the shadow of the ancient castle to which, legend has it, Lancelot fled with his Guinevere. Some say that the recumbent knight lying on the right of the chancel is an effigy of Sir Lancelot du Lac. I'd like to think so – but then, I am a hopeless romantic!

And it's another romantic tale of derring-do that draws many visitors to St Aidan's today. In the graveyard, clearly visible from the sea, stands a memorial to Grace Darling, the Victorian who became a heroine when she was twenty-two. On a stormy night in September 1838, Grace rowed out with her lighthouse-keeper father to rescue survivors from the luxury steamship, *Forfarshire*, which was wrecked off the Farne Islands. Forty-two lives were lost, and the wave of national publicity and attention which followed Grace's courageous and dramatic rescue totally overwhelmed this shy young woman.

Four years later, she died from tuberculosis. Today, her spirit still seems to haunt this windswept churchyard, as she lies in the family grave which looks out over the coastline she knew so well.

Grace is remembered in a stone effigy and a stained-glass window inside the church. But my favourite window in St Aidan's is in St Oswald's Chapel where famous women throughout the ages are remembered, such as Mary, mother of Jesus, Elizabeth Fry, Florence Nightingale, St Elizabeth of Hungary – and St Ursula, the patron saint of 'girls and seamstresses'. Presumably if you are *one*, you should be the *other*!

Most eyecatching of all in this atmospheric church is the chancel, which is surprisingly long, a reminder of the time in the thirteenth century when this was a monastery church and space was needed for the monks. Much later, towards the end of the nineteenth century, a magnificent reredos of carved Caen stone was set up behind the altar, depicting the saints of Northumbria. Names like Aidan, Oswald, Cuthbert and Bede belong to this glorious county, but they sowed the seeds of faith for us

all. The story of Bamburgh's church is at the heart of the story of Christianity in England.

For seventeen years, this parish had been cared for by Reverend Eric Zachau, who welcomes every visitor with the same warmth with which he welcomed me and the *Village Praise* television team some years ago. I've never forgotten the experience. But then with Bamburgh, once visited, never forgotten.

ABOVE:
Memorial to Grace Darling

RIGHT:
Stained-glass window dedicated to Grace

Sinclair Seamen's Presbyterian Church
BELFAST

In the year the Second World War broke out, James Galway was born, the son of a shipbuilder in Belfast Docks. His early family memories of pipe bands and fiddle-playing inspired a love of music which has made him one of the most appreciated flautists in the world. But Jimmy is a man who also has a deep faith and fascination for the Bible, and the seeds of that interest were sown in the Sunday-school class he attended right in the heart of the docks at Sinclair Seamen's Church.

At the time when Jimmy joined other youngsters for Bible classes there every Sunday, Belfast Docks were thriving with a renowned shipbuilding industry, and boats of every kind arriving, loading up and setting off again. Around 1,000 families regularly worshipped at Sinclair Seamen's Church, from a community that was a mixture of both Catholic and Protestant. Today, the docks are quieter, and the old terraced houses have been swept away in favour of smart new flats and commercial developments. But Sinclair Seamen's remains. Wartime bombs missed it, families moved away from it – but it stands stalwart, a cherished and unique Christian oasis as the city of Belfast changes around it.

Once inside, you need no reminder that this building has a special ministry to seamen. From the semaphore flags set into the floor at each door, spelling out 'welcome', to the huge pulpit in the shape of a ship's prow, carved in teak from an old windjammer, the church is so packed with nautical items you can smell the sea salt! A model schooner hangs from the rafters; there are anchor, lifebelt and lighthouse plaques on the walls, and two ships' bells which are regularly rung. Stained-glass windows remember the soldiers, sailors and airmen of the First World War, and the great shipping lines that regularly used Belfast Docks. The brass bell from HMS Hood, the blockship that kept submarines away from the fleet in Portland Harbour during the First World War, is rung at the start of each evening service, and a lighthouse mounted on the wall used to flash until the minister complained that it ruined his concentration during the sermon! One of the barges which regularly carried Guinness along the Liffy in Dublin provided the starboard, port and main mast lights that illuminate the pulpit, and couples getting married stand on an anchor

■ Sinclair Seamen's
Presbyterian Church,
Belfast

set in the floor, in the hope that their marriage will be secure and steadfast. A beautifully renovated solid brass binnacle has often been used for baptisms, and the brass wheel and capstan, which have pride of place at the front of the church, look unrecognisable as the salvage items

they were when they were brought up after five or six years under water from a ship that had sunk off the coast of Scotland during the First World War.

I especially like the collection boxes, which look like lifeboats, replacing the brass rum tot jugs on long poles that used to do the job, which are now

displayed along the wall. And one of the church's favourite ministers, Reverend Samuel Cochrane,

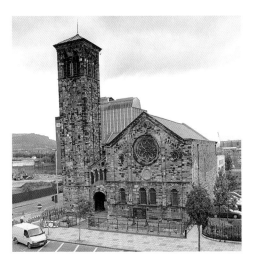

affectionately known as 'Reverend Sam', is commemorated in the porch of the transept, which was erected after his death to stop the draught that he always complained hit his bald spot when he sat in the manse pew!

Jimmy Galway probably recalls Reverend Sam as one of the many colourful memories of his time at this church, which has a thousand tales to tell. It inspired him then, just as it continues to draw, intrigue and inspire today.

F ollow the south shore of the Blackwater Estuary out as far as you can go, and against the backdrop of a huge East Anglian sky you'll come across a stark stone building which has faced the blasts of the North Sea for more than thirteen centuries. Here, as you look across to the nuclear power station at Bradwell which is so much a symbol of our time, the past engulfs you. St Cedd stood here, sent by St Aidan from Lindisfarne in 653. The atmosphere of this remote coastline drew him to establish a Celtic monastic community on this spot, and it is their chapel, steeped now in generations of prayer, that still draws pilgrims today.

It's not surprising that Barbara Erskine, whose novels are read around the world, should find her way to the Chapel of St Peter-on-the-Wall. In her writing, she weaves the essence of Celtic belief into modern-day life, creating stories which are intriguing, powerful and mysterious. Here, in the whistle of the wind, the distant roar of the sea and the

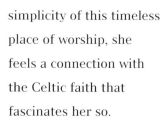

**Chapel of
St Peter-on-
the-Wall**
BRADWELL-ON-SEA,
ESSEX

simplicity of this timeless place of worship, she feels a connection with the Celtic faith that fascinates her so.

When the Romans first came here, towards the end of the third century, they built the Fort of Othona as part of the defence of the Saxon shore. Three hundred years later, St Cedd used some of the stones and tiles from what was left of Othona to build a chapel dedicated to St Peter. This became his cathedral when he was made Bishop of the East Saxons, making the church we see today the earliest cathedral in the country of which so much still remains. Years later, as the population moved inland around a newly built parish church, St Peter's became a chapel of ease, a daughter church, then a lighthouse in Elizabethan times when its tower, now lost, acted as a beacon for ships. Later it became a store for smugglers' booty, and finally a farmer's barn, when huge holes were knocked into the side walls to let farm carts in and out of the building. When the farmer eventually handed the chapel back to the diocese in 1920, it was repaired and renovated, reclaiming the homely solemnity which has drawn visitors in their thousands ever since.

In this ancient place, there are modern touches which are simple and inspiring. The altar is set with three stones in the supporting pillar

Barbara Erskine outside the chapel

representing the communities of Lindisfarne, Iona and Lastingham, all of which featured in St Cedd's ministry. And the cross, high on the wall above the altar, provides the one splash of spectacular colour with its images of St Peter and St Paul.

There is a real sense of pilgrimage as you head towards the chapel along the path that was built by Romans, and walked by saints. To be alongside other worshippers within the walls of St Peter's is wonderful. Better still, come alone, and let the memory and worship of so many before you reach out in fellowship as thoughts and prayers become one.

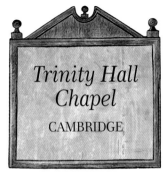

Trinity Hall Chapel

CAMBRIDGE

Cross the River Cam by Clare Bridge, and you'll find yourself in the tangle of winding lanes and roads dividing the elegant academic buildings which make up Cambridge University. Dodging cyclists as you go, make your way to Trinity Hall, one of the oldest and smallest of these ancient establishments, tucked away behind narrow archways that lead to a quiet, colourful courtyard and garden. This is another world, secluded and self-contained, a place to think, write and draw strength – the exact qualities, in fact, that drew Terry Waite here. His long years in captivity had left him physically weak, emotionally scarred and spiritually challenged. This was a haven in which he could slowly come back to life, surrounded by the unobtrusive care of this quietly supportive community.

When Terry was elected as a fellow commoner at Trinity Hall, he recognised the opportunity it offered him to get on with writing his first book, *Taken on Trust*. Reliving the memories of his horrific experience as a hostage of terrorists was painful and cathartic – and ironically his college room facing out onto Trinity Lane even had bars at the window! But only a matter of steps away was the tiny college chapel that became very special to Terry during his fifteen months at Trinity Hall.

As he opened the door leading from the courtyard to the antechapel, he would see two windows celebrating the life of someone who played a crucial part in his own story: the former Archbishop of Canterbury,

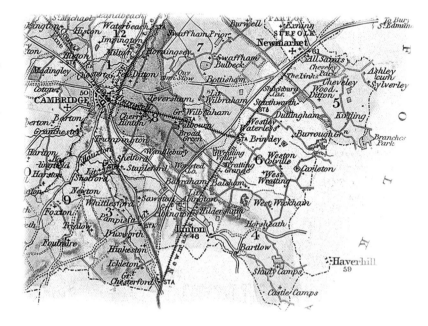

Robert Runcie. Terry was working as the Archbishop's special envoy when he was taken hostage. Runcie had been dean of the college many years earlier, and even famously proposed to his wife Lindy, the daughter of one of the college dons, in the fellows' garden. Their wedding rings, Runcie's military career, his love of cricket and his meeting with Pope John Paul II are all depicted in the circular windows which were installed to mark his elevation to Archbishop of Canterbury.

The chapel itself is tiny and dignified, and was created shortly after the college was founded by Bishop Bateman in the 1350s. Many of the coats of arms which decorate the ceiling bear the crescent that was Bishop Bateman's own emblem.

Behind the altar is a magnificent painting, based on the description of the visitation in St Luke's Gospel, by the sixteenth-century artist Mansuoli, in which, unusually, Mary is dressed in red. This picture originally hung in an Italian church which burned down. Later it was moved to the Vatican, then through Europe to England,

possibly transported on a donkey, as donkey hairs were found on the back of the canvas. It's now on permanent loan to Trinity Hall from the Fitzwilliam Museum in Cambridge, and looks both inspirational and at home in its present surroundings.

Trinity Hall has always had a reputation for specialising in law, but the chapel often welcomes worshippers from beyond its own community of students. With so many grand and beautiful churches to choose from in Cambridge, this small, intimate chapel offers regular Eucharist services, with midday and evening prayer said most days. Best described as Christian, rather than exclusively Anglican, many find here a quiet oasis for private moments of thought and prayer.

It was certainly the place where Terry found the peace he needed to start laying the ghosts of the past to rest, and to gather strength for the future. When it was time to leave Trinity Hall, he left behind two emotive momentoes of his time in captivity. The first was the chipped magnifying glass with which he was sometimes able to read. The second was the blindfold which he always had to wear whenever anyone came into his cell. Because Trinity Hall and its chapel contributed so much to the process of his healing, Terry was able to walk away from these graphic reminders of what he'd been through – and move on.

Terry Waite beside the Robert Runcie windows

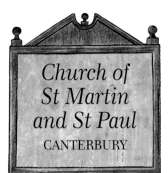

Church of St Martin and St Paul
CANTERBURY

'Here they first assembled to sing the psalms, to pray, to say Mass, to preach and to baptise, until the king's own conversion to the Faith gave them greater freedom to preach and to build and restore churches everywhere.'

What a wonderful sense of history these words of the Venerable Bede provide for today's congregation at St Martin's in Canterbury, probably the oldest parish church in England – a tiny building with a huge place in the story of our faith in this country.

This was the church in which St Augustine of Canterbury, sent to England by Pope Gregory the Great, first preached and worshipped. It was from this humble base that his monks and followers travelled north, spreading the gospel as they went. St Martin's had been the obvious starting point, because it was the private chapel of Queen Bertha, who had been promised a place of Christian worship when she arrived here to marry King Ethelbert. She named her chapel after the monk who had inspired her so much in the French city of Tours, Bishop Martin, who, according to legend, tore his cloak in half to comfort a beggar, only to have it revealed in a dream that the beggar was Christ himself.

Standing quite literally in the shadow of Canterbury Cathedral, St Martin's has been the private favourite of many Archbishops – and our present Archbishop of Canterbury, George Carey, is no exception. I shall never forget the anniversary in 1997 of the arrival of St Augustine to these shores 1,400 years ago, and the grand cathedral service to which royalty and church leaders from around the world were invited. I reached Canterbury early, and with about an hour to fill, noticed that worshippers were going into St Martin's for the Sunday-morning service, and decided to join them. To my surprise, the tiny church was packed to bursting, because the sermon that day was by the Archbishop himself! This was George Carey where he is most at home,

*A quiet moment for
Archbishop George Carey*

speaking from the heart in the intimate setting of a parish church. For me, it was a revealing insight into the man who hours later was leading worship for the nation in the televised service from the cathedral.

Run your fingers across the Roman wall tiles near the remains of the door

■ CHURCH OF
ST MARTIN AND ST PAUL,
Canterbury

through which Queen Bertha probably came to worship, and while you're near the altar, note the unusual and haunting cross, fashioned in wrought iron, a replica of the piece of driftwood used for some years after the original brass cross was stolen in the 1970s. The font has an intricate design of interlocking rings, and was probably moved to St Martin's from the nearby priory, rather than being the baptismal font of King Ethelbert, as legend has it. And don't miss the small display case in the wall which houses a medieval copper-alloy chrismatory, which would have contained three holy oils. Most of these containers were melted down in Elizabethan times as part of a campaign against superstition, so that only pure metals could then be used in church.

But my favourite spot is in the graveyard, where you can stand on a raised mound of grass and look out on one of the very best views of the cathedral city. St Augustine may have stood here too, watching as the good news of the gospel was taken from this cradle of Christianity to the rest of England.

Chapel of St Christopher's Hospice

SYDENHAM, SOUTH LONDON

Every morning at quarter to nine, Dame Cicely Saunders joins a small gathering to pray in the chapel of St Christopher's Hospice, not far from the south circular in London. As chapels go, this one looks as if it could quite easily become a canteen or an office area. It is a long plain room lined by windows which look out on the car park. Beyond the door, you hear the comings and goings of the hospice: the banging of pots in the kitchen, greetings in the corridor, the distant ringing of telephones, the sound of laughter. But here, in this flexible, down-to-earth room with its lovingly arranged flowers, you feel the almost tangible presence of God.

That has been the experience of so many who have made their way to this room in the years since St Christopher's opened its doors in 1967, at that time for fifty-four patients needing terminal care. This hospice was the realisation of a much-cherished vision for Dame Cicely, who, firstly as a nurse, then as a social worker, and finally as a doctor, had recognised the need for patients to face death with dignity, in the care of skilled, caring staff with time for the individual. Her practical, compassionate approach to palliative care, especially in the provision of pain control, established a new era in the care of the dying. Without the burden of pain, people are able to 'live until the moment they die', allowing them the opportunity to tidy up loose ends, right old wrongs, give thanks and say goodbyes.

For many patients, and their families too, there is also the wish to look ahead to what lies beyond death – and it is that which often takes them to the chapel. Not all of them are Christian. Some are from other faiths. Many have no faith at all. Death, though, is a leveller of men, and this quiet dignified room, with its simple cherrywood cross, feels like the right place to ask life's big questions: Why? How can a loving God allow us to suffer in this way? When my loved one dies, how do I know that God will be there for them? Many families return a year after their loss for a thanksgiving and memorial service in the chapel, when their eyes are no doubt drawn to the three stunning paintings on the side wall by Dame Cicely's late husband, Marian Bohusz, a talented Polish artist. His interpretations of the incarnation, crucifixion and resurrection exude the pain, grief and hope which is mirrored so often in the emotions of those who come to pray here. It is a place of peace and sanctity in the middle of this inspiring, busy building – just as death has its place in the midst of life.

LEFT:
Incarnation, Crucifixion and Resurrection *by Marian Bohusz*

LEFT:
Dame Cicely Saunders, founder of the hospice movement

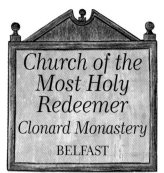

Church of the Most Holy Redeemer
Clonard Monastery
BELFAST

This beautiful, unassuming church is one of the most inspiring I've ever visited. It stands on Falls Road in West Belfast, on the dividing line between the Catholic community and their Protestant neighbours in Shankill Road. This is an area which has ignited with hatred and intolerance over the years, and Clonard couldn't help but be caught in the political and sectarian crossfire. But for the congregation, and the Redemptorists for whom the monastery has been home for more than a century, their location has been both a blessing and an incentive. Working towards peace and reconciliation is right at the heart of their mission, an apostolic priority of the Redemptorist community – and over the years that mission has taken them into challenging, emotional and sometimes dangerous situations. Against a background of violence, murder and destruction, Clonard has held out a hand of Christian friendship across the divide, to meet the outstretched hand of Christians in the Protestant denominations.

Strangely enough, one of the best views of the church, which was built in early French Gothic style soon after the turn of the nineteenth century, comes from the Shankill side. For years its grey towers have peered down on the barbed wire and tightly packed houses that are gradually being cleared away as modernisation and a newly realistic hope of peace take hold. But the rather colourless exterior simply doesn't prepare you for the richly glorious interior, breathtaking in the way it combines scale and grandeur with warmth and intimacy. Traditional and beautifully crafted images of the redemption of Christ, depicted in a semicircular crown of mosaics high in the nave, sit comfortably alongside the remodelled sanctuary, which has a more modern feel. Here the bronze ambo with a dove symbolising the Holy Spirit, the white American oak chair, the stone altar, and a golden-orange high-altar tapestry representing the brightness of God's glory, are ranged at rising

36

levels along the central line of the church. Loveliest of all is Our Lady's Shrine, which is small, ornate and lined with flowers in every array from small bunches to brides' bouquets, each bloom representing a prayer.

A church, though, is not a building but a people – and many of those who fill the pews for Mass on Sunday have followed the example of the brothers in wanting to know more about the community and church of their Protestant neighbours across the divide, exploring the differences, while recognising their common belief in Christ which unites them. That ecumenical spirit has quietly flourished for years in this corner of Belfast, and flowered in the

establishment of the multi-denominational Cornerstone Community on the Springfield Road peace-line, and 'Forthspring' at Springfield Road Methodist Church where Catholics and Protestants now come together in a variety of projects. These are both initiatives with which Clonard has been closely involved. There are also many occasions now in Clonard Church when Catholics and Protestants worship together. For them, the longing for peace on earth has heartfelt meaning, as through prayer, understanding and God's grace they work together to make that peace a reality.

**Friends'
Meeting House
Come-to-Good**
TRURO, CORNWALL

There is such a variety of churches in this book, from the grand and glorious to the ancient and atmospheric – but there are few which made more impression on me than this little house of God in a tiny Cornish hamlet which you could blink and miss. The simple thatched building, where Quakers have gathered for centuries to still the clamour of everyday life and sense the eternal through silent worship, is both compelling and inspiring.

Some say that Come-to-Good was given its delightful name because of the Friends meeting there, and if so there was irony in the choice of title. When George Fox, the founder of the Quakers, came to Cornwall in 1656 bringing his revolutionary message that no intermediary or ritual was needed in order for us to have an individual relationship with God, he was arrested and thrown into the horror pit known as Doomsdale in Launceston Castle. Church and state were hard to separate at that time, and people were not only expected to attend parish worship, but also to give financial support in the form of tithes. Fox's followers felt that the gift of ministry could not be bought or sold – and their views landed many of them in trouble, scorned by their neighbours and tormented by the authorities.

Memories of that stormy start to the Quaker movement seem distant as you stand in this peaceful setting today. Before it was levelled in the 1950s, the land around the house was bumpy with the unmarked graves of generations of local Friends. Since then, each season of the year brings colour and pleasure as wild flowers such as primroses, daffodils, columbines, bluebells and wild orchids burst into bloom.

This is the only grade-one-listed chapel in Cornwall, and it was built in 1710 with thick cob walls and thatch which sits like huge eyebrows over the windows. In Cornwall, thatched roofs like this one are traditionally made of wheat rather than the more common reeds used elsewhere in the country. Over the years, the thatch

■ FRIENDS' MEETING HOUSE,
*Come-to-Good,
Truro, Cornwall*

has taken on a coating of lichen which adds a charming green hue to the roof – although 'charming' may not be the word the current Friends would choose! To one side is the linhay, or haystore, where you can almost imagine horses waiting in years gone by. There are mounting steps still to be seen, once used by those with large horses and short legs! Inside, the homely square room is lined with simple wooden benches, looked down upon by the gallery, which was added in 1717 for the princely sum of fifteen pounds and ten shillings. Quite perplexing is the door to one side of the gallery which goes nowhere except down onto the Friends below. This was, in fact, the previous entrance to the gallery before the stairs were moved some years ago.

Modernisation discreetly crept in, though, when the old porch was replaced and extended in the late 1960s to add a kitchen and young

people's area. Until then, youngsters had met in the children's room, an old stable block a few yards away from the main building.

Three thousand visitors a year make their way here to look round this unique little building. I'm sure they all find, as I did, that an atmosphere of peace and worship surrounds them the moment they walk in the door. Come-to-Good may not have the splendour of a grand cathedral, or the large congregation of a busy parish church, but in its simplicity, and the warm sincerity of the Quaker Friends who welcome you in, you will find God.

Andrew Lloyd Webber has a great love of old churches, so much so that he established and supports the Open Churches Trust to keep church doors open for visitors. Of the sixty or so buildings now supported by the trust, I have chosen two favourites of mine in Derbyshire: the Chapel of St Mary on the Bridge in the centre of Derby, which is covered in the next section, and All Saints' Church, Dale Abbey, which is one of the most unusual and charming churches I have ever discovered.

'Semi-detached des. res.' is,

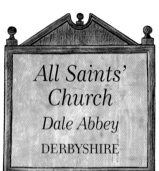

I suppose, how an estate agent would describe this honey-coloured building, which is half church and half farmhouse. The division came about in 1485, when the monks at the nearby abbey decided to convert half of the structure into an infirmary, leaving the rest as the infirmary chapel. There were connecting doors both on the ground and gallery floors, where even today you can see the low platforms on which the sick could be laid on stretchers in a position to see the pulpit. And the pulpit is certainly worth seeing! It's a triple-decker affair, combined with the priest's and clerk's stalls, which lean alarmingly to one side, balanced by the floor which seems to lean conveniently to the other! They are all grouped around a communion table, which is actually a Jacobean cupboard in which the silver and robes used to be stored. Just as well it's a fairly big cupboard, because the chalice in this tiny chapel is reputed to be the biggest in England, some nine inches high and fifteen inches around the rim!

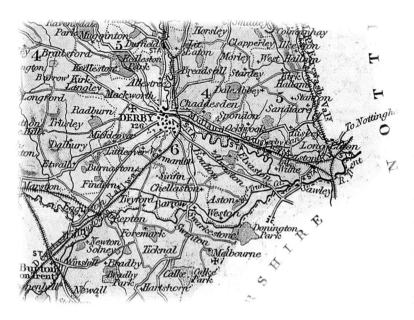

But what it lacks in space, All Saints' makes up for in character, built on centuries of loving use. In fact, the locals around here have always made excellent use of the building, especially when, for a while, it was a combination of chapel and pub! The clergy used to put on their robes in the inn, then walk through the door for the service, before returning to quench their thirst after their devotions! And even during the service, the minister couldn't have been sure he had the complete attention of his congregation as the box pews in the interior, which hasn't altered since around 1650, are arranged so that you can sit with

your back to the pulpit and nod off gently!

After the dissolution of the abbey in 1538 the chapel became a 'peculiar', meaning that the rights of bishop over the little church passed to the person who bought it. There was also a court here which had the authority to issue licences for weddings without banns being read, so, in the seventeenth century, All Saints' Church became the Gretna Green of the Midlands. What a lovely setting for a wedding – even if the aisle is so narrow that the groom has to stand behind the bride!

■ ALL SAINTS' CHURCH, *Dale Abbey, Derbyshire*

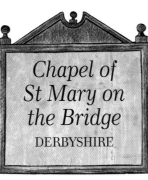

**Chapel of
St Mary on
the Bridge**

DERBYSHIRE

Drivers thundering across the inner ring-road flyover in the centre of Derby probably barely notice the jumble of gables and mullioned windows to their left, within which stands a rare treasure – one of the few surviving bridge chapels in England. There has been a chapel beside the River Derwent since the end of the thirteenth century, by which time the bridge was built of stone, replacing the wooden structure that probably dated back to Saxon times. For centuries, travel was a precarious business, and the opportunity to receive a blessing or offer a prayer – or peer through the squint at the side of the chapel which even today gives a view of the altar area and possibly the sacrament – was a reassuring necessity before the traveller left the safety of the town for the unknown countryside beyond. In fact, though, the chapel did more than just nurture the spirit. It fed the coffers, too, because tolls were regularly collected here to pay for the upkeep of the bridge.

Over the years, this chapel has played many roles. In the fourteenth century, a cell was created to house an anchoress, a woman who had withdrawn from the world to live in silence and prayer. A hundred years later, when twelve lady benefactors had banded together to form the Sisters of Our Lady and Child of the Bridge, a much-revered figure known as the Black Virgin of Derby was elaborately displayed on high days and holidays, making this a pilgrimage site in the area. By the middle of the sixteenth century, when Catholic Mary had been succeeded by Protestant Elizabeth, three Catholic priests were hung, drawn and quartered here, with their bodies displayed around the entrance of the chapel. To this day, their death is remembered in a joint ecumenical service shared by the Anglicans, who now care for the chapel under their vicar, the provost of Derby, and their Roman Catholic neighbours from the splendid church just up the hill.

The symbol of a church on a bridge

drawing sides together suits this small chapel well, because in recent years it has opened its doors to welcome a variety of Christian communities. The German Lutheran and Latvian congregations still worship there regularly, and although there is no longer a Lithuanian congregation, on two Sundays of each month services are held by a Russian Orthodox congregation, who fill the tiny atmospheric church with icons and candles.

The modern altar, designed in Derbyshire stone by a local architect in the 1970s, is quaintly at odds with the mixture of treasures here. I enjoyed climbing the winding stairs to the gallery, almost filled by a grand piano, from which you can look down on a congregation who would have to be very neighbourly to fit in more

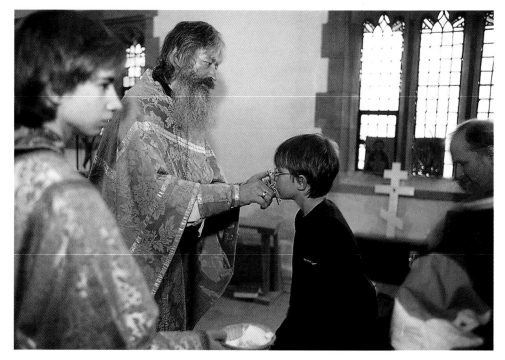

St Christopher

47

than thirty-five at a time. The windows are worth close inspection too, the one standing behind the altar being especially moving. It's dedicated to the memory of Sean Ferguson, who died from cancer in 1972 at the age of just twenty-one, and contains images associated with Mary, mother of Jesus, such as the lily, swallow and unicorn, symbols of virginity. See if you can spot the cat, representing the charming legend of the puss who gave birth to a litter of kittens in the stable in Bethlehem on the night of the nativity – and the caterpillar, cocoon and butterfly that was Sean's

favourite metaphor of death and resurrection.

The fabric of this chapel is steeped in a simplicity and presence that tell of generations of worship and community life spanning the centuries – and in the heart of a modern city, this is a treasure worth finding.

ABOVE:
Stained-glass window dedicated to Sean Ferguson

LEFT:
Russian Orthodox icons

There is a tradition that where two rivers meet is a holy place. The Druids thought so, and long before Christianity reached our shores, they held ceremonies on the north bank of the mighty River Tay at the point where it meets the River Braan, surrounded by the Perthshire hills and sheltered by forest trees. St Columba of Iona felt the pull of this place, too, and chose it as a headquarters around 570 AD for his disciples, or 'Culdees' ('friends of God') – although that choice probably had less to do with atmosphere and more to do with Dunkeld's strategic position on the borders of North and South Pictland.

The Culdees' church, which was probably made of mud and wattle, was rebuilt in stone in 848 by Kenneth MacAlpin, who became the first King of the Scots, once he had united the Picts with their neighbours in the west of Scotland in 844. Legend has it that the King brought St Columba's relics here from Iona for safe keeping from marauding Norsemen, and the belief that the saint's bones were buried under the chancel steps has made the cathedral dedicated to his memory a place of pilgrimage ever since.

Scotland's turbulent history has often been reflected in the fate of Dunkeld Cathedral. In medieval times, it became the centre of power for a number of bishops who combined their pastoral duties with a leading role in the government and administration of the kingdom. It helped the King to have a sympathetic Bishop in place at Dunkeld, although stories abound of disputes and power-bargaining between the crown and the clerics. In later years, the cathedral was twice desecrated and almost destroyed. In 1560, following the Reformation, the Privy Council issued an order to local lairds to destroy 'images of idolatry'. They interpreted this order freely as an excuse for widespread destruction, tearing off the roof, stealing furnishings and smashing the stained-glass windows. Then in 1689, during the Battle of Dunkeld, when most of the town was devastated by fire, government troops in the tower used wood from the cathedral as barricades and lead from what was left of the roof as shot. Although some renovation work was done to the choir in the years that followed, it wasn't until 1908 that it was restored as near as possible to its original form as the result of a fortunate and heart-warming meeting. At that time, the building and the surrounding land were owned by the Duke of Atholl, who only allowed the minister, Reverend Thomas

The ruins of Dunkeld Cathedral remaining today

Rutherford, and his parishioners access to the church for thirty minutes before and after a service. Requests to be more lenient had fallen on deaf ears. However, fate had it that the minister's daughter Margaret was nursing in Glen Lyon at the time, where her patient was the rich industrialist Sir Donald Currie. When he recovered from the illness he had thought would kill him, he asked Margaret what he could do to show his gratitude for her care. She suggested he might help her father restore the cathedral at Dunkeld – and that is exactly what he did. He brought in the very best architects and craftsmen to put up the beautiful oak roof, renew the pews and carved screen around the communion table,

and replace the stained-glass east window depicting St Columba, the shepherds receiving the Christmas message and the Christian values of faith, hope and charity. And once the cathedral was so splendidly restored, the duke was quite happy to welcome visitors there!

What we see at Dunkeld today is a splendid church, worthy of its ancestry of powerful abbots and bishops, standing alongside the atmospheric remains of the rest of the cathedral, which has been in ruins since its destruction four centuries ago. The dignity of its huge arches, the grimacing of the 'green man' gargoyles that beam down from its walls, the forlorn beauty of what was once a lovely pointed west window, the tall bell tower where courts sat in judgement beneath medieval wall-paintings of parables to remind them of the need for justice with fairness, all combine to make Dunkeld Cathedral a church shaped not just by the devotion of generations of worshippers, but by the twists and turns of Scottish history.

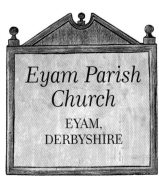

'Ring a ring of roses,
A pocket full of posies,
Atishoo, atishoo,
We all fall down.'

D o you remember singing this much-loved children's rhyme when you were a youngster? It sounds delightful and harmless, but in fact its origins date back to one of the most tragic times in England's history, and in particular to the pain-filled past of a small parish church in the Derbyshire Dales.

In September 1665, as bubonic plague was taking grip in the South of England, a box of cloth was delivered from London to the tailor in the village of Eyam. The fleas in the cloth were contaminated, and days later the tailor died. Within fifteen months, 276 of the village's 350 inhabitants were also dead.

Right at the heart of that devastated community was the parish church dedicated to St Lawrence, with its recently appointed young rector, William Mompesson. Recognising the danger of an epidemic spreading throughout the North of England, Mompesson persuaded his

Eyam Parish Church

EYAM, DERBYSHIRE

parishioners to shut themselves off with the plague, knowing that for many of them it would be a death sentence. Food could be left at collection points on the edge of the village, and paid for with coins disinfected in vinegar. Prayer took on even more poignant meaning in the face of fear, illness and bereavement, but when Mompesson realised that services in the church could increase the spread of disease, he continued to lead worship in a nearby field at Cucklett Delf for his desperate, dwindling congregation.

Mompesson's record in the parish register makes for grim reading, as whole families were wiped out. Saddest of all is one of the final entries from that period: the death of the rector's devoted wife Catherine. Her table tomb stands today in the graveyard, a symbol of the love and self-sacrifice at the heart of the story of St Lawrence's and its parishioners.

This church has been dear to me for more than twenty years, ever since, as a very new presenter, I spent a week in Eyam along with actors, dozens of

■ EYAM PARISH CHURCH,
Eyam, Derbyshire

extras and a huge television crew, who were recreating those seventeenth-century events. I shall never forget, as I ran my finger down the original register where Mompesson's own hand had recorded so many deaths, how moved I was at the tragedy and selflessness of Eyam. That register is now kept safely in Matlock, but a copy is on show in the church, along with a plague cupboard said to have been made from the box which carried the original bale of cloth.

BELOW:
Parish record of deaths
from the plague

John Torre · 29	Brigett Naylour · 13	Mary Darby · 4
Samuel Pealott · 29	Robt Hadfeild · 14	William Abell · 7
Rowland Mower (Senior) 29	Margaret Swinerton · 14	George Fryth · 7
Thomas Bockinge · 30	Alice Coyle · 14	Godfry Ashe · 8
Nicholas Whitley · 30	Thurston Whitley · 15	William Hawksworth · 9
Jonathan Talbot · 30	Alice Bockinge · 15	Robert Wood · 9
Mary Whytley · 30	Brigett Talbott · 15	Humphry Merrell · 9
Rowland Mower (Samuel) 30	Michael Kempe · 15	Sarah Wilson · 10
Robert Kempe · 30	Anne Wilson · 15	Thomas Mosley · 16
Sarah Pealott · 31	Thomas Bilston · 16	Joan Wood · 16
Joseph Alleyn · 31	Thomas Fryth · 17	Mary Percival · 18
Anne Morten · 31	Joan French · 17	Francis Morten · 20
	Mary Pealott · 17	George Butterworth · 21
George Ashe (August 1.1666)	Sarah Morten · 18	Anne Townend · 22
Mary Mealour · 1	Elizabeth Fryth · 18	Anne Glover · 23
John Hadfeild · 2	Anne Pealott · 18	Anne Hall · 23
Robert Buxton · 2	Thomas Ragge · 18	Francis Hawksworth · 23
Anne Naylour · 2		Townend (an Infant) · 29
Jonathan Naylour · 2		Susanna Morten · 29
Elizabeth Glover · 2		
Alexander Hadfeild · 3		Jonas Parsley (October. 1. 1666)
Jane Mealour · 3		Grace Morten · 2
Godfry Torre · 3		Peter Ashe · 4
John Hancocke, (Junior) · 3		Abraham Morten · 5
Elizabeth Hancocke · 3		Thomas Torre (Senior)
Margaret Buxton · 3		Benjamin Morten
Robert Bockinge · 3		Elizabeth Morten
Margaret Percivall · 4	Anne Hawksworth (August.19.1666)	Alice Taylour
Anne Swinerton · 4	Joan Ashemore · 19	Anne Parsley (no dates given.)
Rebeccah Morten · 4	Elizabeth Fryth · 20	Agnes Sheldon
Robert French · 6	Margaret Morten · 20	Mary Morten
Richard Thorpe · 6	Anne Rowland · 20	Samuel Hall
Thomas Fryth · 6	Joan Buxton · 20	Peter Hall
John Pealott · 7	Francis Fryth · 21	Joseph Morten
Oner Hancocke · 7	Ruth Morten · 21	Grace Morten · 15
John Hancocke · 7	Fryth (an Infant) · 21	Elizabeth Danyell · 17
William Hancocke (his son) · 7	Lydia Kempe · 22	Anne Grundy · 17
Abraham Swinerton · 8	Peter Hall · 23	Francis Morten · 18
Alice Hancocke · 9	Morten (an Infant) · 24	William Morten · 28
Anne Hancocke · 10	Katherine Mompesson · 25	
	Samuel Chapman · 25	Abraham Morten (November. 1. 1666.)
Frances Fryth · 10	Anne Fryth · 25	
Elizabeth Kempe · 11	Joan Howe · 27	Eyam Village
William Hawksworth · 12	Thomas Ashemore · 27	The population at commencement
Thomas Kempe · 12	Thomas Wood · 28	of the Plague is given as 350.
Francis Bockinge · 13	William Howe · 30	Only 83 Survived.
	Mary Abell · 30	
	Katherine Talbott · 30	

55

Inside the church, look out for Mompesson's chair, the plague window commissioned in 1985, and a small spider's web in the corner of the window near the main door, the trademark of its designer, Christopher Webb. Once outside, cast your eye over the eighth-century celtic cross, the correction of a spelling mistake on Catherine Mompesson's tomb, and the magnificent sundial which shows the time in Derbyshire as well as that in several cities around the world.

Not that you'd want to be anywhere else. Derbyshire in general, and Eyam Parish Church in particular, are hard to rival.

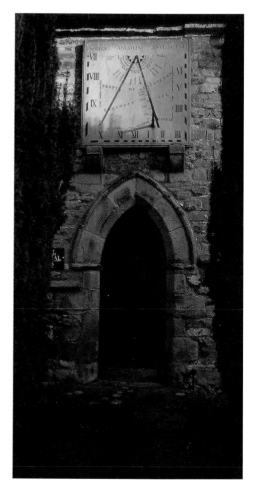

RIGHT:
Catherine Mompesson's tomb, complete with corrected spelling mistake!

Take the road south from Hereford, and just before you reach Ross-on-Wye, only a short distance away from the Welsh border, turn off the road for a couple of miles to find a touch of Tuscany! Pick a day of bright sunshine, and, as you climb up the narrow steps towards the grand rosy-coloured tower of St Catherine's Church, this could be a mountain village in Italy. Savour that thought as you walk through the arched colonnade with its mosaic flooring; you'll then find it's quite a surprise to look down across the graveyard which tumbles away to be surrounded by a cluster of houses with the unmistakeable feel of a British village.

St Catherine's didn't always look like this. It was built in 1840, not as a parish church, but as a chapel of rest, in a style which meant it was later described as 'an ugly brick building with no pretensions to any style of architecture'. That was the opinion of prebendary William Poole, the vicar from 1854, who decided to beautify

his church after he came into a fortune from property he owned in the North of England. Whether he chose this continental style because he'd done the Grand Tour, we'll probably never know. Whatever his reason, he and his architect friend Seddon created a masterpiece. They started by coating the original walls with soft pink sandstone, while the interior design was inspired by the Cathedral of Le Puy in France, with many of the carvings copied from San Vitale at Ravenna in Italy. The outer cloister is like Laon Cathedral in France, with marble brought from France and Cornwall to create the four central pillars which support the ceiling of the domed apse. The pulpit of white and green marble is very similar to the one found at Fiesole Cathedral near Florence, and the hanging lamps may remind you of those you'll see in Venice at St Mark's Church, except for one small detail: the lions are no longer holding books. These were cut off by thieves hoping to disguise the lamps after they stole them in 1974. It didn't work because the thieves were discovered at Dover, and the lamps returned, bookless, to their rightful place.

The white marble altar, with its tiger's-eye cross, is flanked on one side by beautifully carved choir stalls crowned with statues not, as you might expect, of continental saints, but of Welsh ones – a recognition of the Celtic heritage of this community which lives so close to the border between England and Wales.

There is a tangible feeling of presence in this elegant little church – perhaps a little too much for some of the locals! Story has it that during one service, when no organist was available, the minister asked the congregation to sing unaccompanied –

St Catherine's
Church,
*Hoarwithy,
Herefordshire*

and at least three worshippers distinctly heard the organ playing along during the last hymn!

Some delightful local traditions are continued at St Catherine's, like the Eucharist service on Maundy Thursday during which the Office of Tenebrae is celebrated. Nine candles lit on the altar are extinguished one by one during nine readings telling the events of Maundy Thursday. Eventually, the church is completely dark and movingly silent, until one candle is lit again to signify the light and hope of Christ's resurrection.

Another local custom shared by several churches in the area is the giving of pax cakes for Palm Sunday. These are shortbread biscuits, probably accompanied by a cup of tea nowadays rather than the traditional ale, for promoting 'peace and good neighbourhood' between the parishes – which adds to the feeling of welcome you'll find in this friendly, beautiful corner of the country.

Patrick Lichfield is a man with an eye for form and beauty. As one of the world's best-known and respected photographers, he has captured unforgettable images of beauty, personality and occasion. So when Patrick mentioned that his favourite church is a tiny gem belonging to his neighbour, Lord Shrewsbury, just a few miles from his own ancestral home at Shugborough, I couldn't resist a visit. I wasn't disappointed – and neither will you be if you manage to see it for yourself.

Here, in this out-of-the-way Staffordshire village, you find a little masterpiece which is a scaled-down

St Mary the Virgin
INGESTRE,
STAFFORDSHIRE

version of a church you would expect to see in London. If it brings to mind echoes of St Paul's, St Bride's in Fleet Street or St Martin's in Ludgate, that's not surprising, because the designer of this church of St Mary the Virgin was none other than Christopher Wren himself. St Mary's was first used for worship in 1676, a year before work started on the building of St Paul's. In so many ways, this church at Ingestre was the prototype for beautiful ideas carried further in the great churches of London, such as the clusters of angel heads over the arches as seen in St Paul's, the medieval style of layout for the nave and aisles as used in St Bride's, the tower with balustrade and arms later seen at St Andrew's in Holborn, and the Tuscan order of the doorway, which also appears in Trinity College Library in Cambridge.

St Mary's was the family church on the estate of Sir Walter Chetwynd, and Wren's interest in its rebuilding grew from the friendship between the two men during their time together at Oxford. Walter's wife and baby had died, and it's thought that he wanted this beautiful church to be a memorial to them. Surely the fact that the church was moved from its original site, which meant re-routing the planned new road to Stafford away from the front of the family hall, had nothing to do with his decision to rebuild! The design was unique then, because it featured a chancel at a time when chancels were definitely 'out'. Beneath it is the crypt, with a family tomb at the east end in which Walter reburied the bodies of ancestors that

Lord Lichfield
at the door of
St Mary the Virgin

had been removed from the earlier church. Over the years, apart from the immediate family, four others are believed to have been buried in the tomb, including a much-loved estate worker, Harry Hancocks, who died in his nineties – and a lady 'housekeeper' who moved into the hall shortly before the First World War, to stay with the earl of the time who was no longer living with his wife. Later, the earl's son refused to take his rightful place in the family tomb because he objected to this lady being there among his ancestors!

When St Mary's was opened in August 1676, seven sacraments were

enacted on the first day: early-morning communion, morning prayer, evensong, a wedding, a funeral, a baptism and the churching of a woman who had recently given birth.

A little over 200 years later, in 1886, St Mary's became only the second church in the country to have electric light fitted, a claim to fame particularly remembered recently as the church has just been totally rewired, and the ceilings illuminated by new lighting. This means that the intricacies of the crowning glories of the church are even easier to see, such as the beautiful carvings by a young Grindling Gibbons at the start of his career. His touch is unmistakable – just as the head of Sir Christopher Wren he carved onto the screen is instantly recognisable.

St Mary's, Ingestre, is a wonderful surprise in this quiet corner of England, a church that brings together the finest talent of the land in a perfect country setting. The detail, symmetry and craftsmanship draw the eye and lift the soul.

And with his eye for beautiful things, no wonder Lord Lichfield loves it!

**Hospital of
St Cross**

WINCHESTER

If you're ever in Winchester, take time to pay a visit to the Hospital of St Cross, the ancient almshouses and church established by William the Conqueror's grandson, Henry de Blois, who became Bishop of Winchester. Legend has it that one day, when Henry was walking in the Itchen meadows, he was stopped by a young girl with a pail of milk on her head and a baby in her arms. She begged the Bishop to help her people who were starving because of the civil war. The parallel with Mary, mother of Jesus, was all too clear to De Blois – and when, further on, he saw the ruins at Sparkford of a former religious house destroyed by the Danes, he resolved to set up a community there to help the poor.

Originally, his plan was to house 'thirteen poor men, feeble and reduced in strength', and to provide a 'dinner each day for 100 other poor persons' – and in essence that tradition still remains. It was enhanced three centuries later in the 1440s when Cardinal Henry Beaufort established his Foundation for the Almshouses of Noble Poverty, which probably in the early years particularly helped those finding themselves in reduced circumstances through taking up with the wrong side during the Wars of the Roses. Beaufort built the square of houses we see today, where twenty-five gentlemen brothers now live, still wearing the traditional gowns that have been their hallmark for centuries – black in memory of De Blois, and mulberry for Cardinal Beaufort. An essential part of their daily duty is to attend morning service in the glorious Norman church, the nave of which was originally crowned with a thatched roof. Like the cathedral just a couple of miles down the road, this church feared the arrival of the Puritans during the Reformation, so the congregation pushed their altar stone back against the wall, where it was plastered in for centuries before being restored to its former position in 1928. At the same time, the lectern was cut in two, and hidden in a grave

down the road at St Faith's Church. One
of the panels above the Red Brothers'
stalls bears the carved head of Anne
Boleyn. Legend has it that this panel
was removed from above the bed in
Wolvesey Palace where Henry VIII was
due to sleep, just after he'd chopped
off Anne's head. Perhaps fearing for
his own neck, the Bishop decided
to remove her effigy rather than
offend him!

In far-off days, St Cross stood on
an important east–west route. Pedlars
with pack mules and pilgrims on
ponies ambled through the water
meadows to break their journey at
the hospital, resting tired steeds and
weary feet. There they could request
the wayfarer's dole, in those days a
bottle of wine and a loaf of bread, to
help them on their journey. Today,
when lorries and cars thunder past on

the nearby M3, the tradition remains –
although visitors who request the
dole now are given a more modest
mouthful of bread and a small cup of
beer – and a reminder not to drink
and drive!

St Lawrence's Church

HUNGERFORD

I shall never forget my first glimpse of this church. It was a glorious summer's day, and I was gliding along the Kennet and Avon Canal, filming on a narrowboat which had been specially converted to be suitable for people with disabilities. Just as we reached the point where someone had to leap out to open the swing bridge, St Lawrence's Church loomed into view through a veil of graceful trees, its Bath-stone walls glowing pink in the sunlight.

There is an air of solidity about this church which belies its real age. Although there has been Christian worship on this spot for the best part of 1,000 years, the present building has been standing for little more than a century and a half. The Normans probably built the first church here, and its later Gothic replacement collapsed in the early 1800s just as the parishioners were busy fundraising to repair and improve the building. In the end, between 1814 and 1816, the remainder of the ancient church was demolished and cleared away, and an architect commissioned to model St Lawrence's on one of the elegant churches in the Bath area. It was at this stage that the Avon and Kennet Canal really came into its own. It had never been very successful as a commercial waterway as the railway arrived before its completion, but the little rural canal was put to good use ferrying the Bath stone slabs along to the building site.

Later, towards the end of the nineteenth century, the enthusiasm and organising skills of the vicar of the time, Reverend James Anstice, led to some tasteful change and renovation: the roof was raised, new pillars constructed, pews replaced and the heating and lighting improved. One delightful addition was the carving of angel figures around the main supports of the roof, each bearing either the arms of the town, or the grid-iron symbol of St Lawrence, who'd met a grisly end being roasted as a martyr. James Anstice, whose sight became poor in later life, is remembered in the

stained-glass window that shows Jesus healing a blind man, and the shallow semicircle surrounding the altar is bathed in soft light from the unusual rounded east window depicting the theme of 'feed my sheep'. The other end of the building is dominated by a magnificent array of organ pipes, showily painted to conceal the fact that the organ is probably past its best, especially as many of the pipes are false anyway!

There are some intriguing

memorials lining the walls, such as the one for poor Henry Cundell who was just twenty-four years old when he was struck down by lightning in 1864; another for Percy Richens, the wirelessman on board a submarine which was blown up by an Allied mine in 1918; and the plaque remembering William Cheyney and his wife who were 'barbarously murdered in their own house' just before Christmas in 1762. Most touching of all is the simple, discreet plaque remembering

the more recent tragedy in Hungerford in 1987, when Michael Ryan killed sixteen local people before turning the gun on himself.

But for the visitor, it is the approach and the exterior of this church that give most pleasure. Arrive on a narrowboat, and bring a picnic with you, so that you can sit on the bank and watch the world sail by St Lawrence's in this unspoilt corner of England.

ABOVE:
Memorial to 'the men of Hungerford who fell in the Great Wars'.

LEFT:
East window

Italian Chapel
LAMBHOLM, THE ORKNEYS

During the Second World War, several hundred Italian prisoners of war, mostly reluctant soldiers, were captured in North Africa and shipped to the Orkneys, the islands stretching away from the very north of Scotland. From a nation of accomplished builders, these prisoners were the right people for the task of constructing the Churchill Barriers, the massive series of concrete causeways needed to seal the eastern approaches to Scapa Flow – although at the time they were cunningly disguised as 'roadways' because, under the terms of the Geneva Convention, PoWs were not allowed to work on wartime defences.

The climate and conditions proved tough for these marooned continentals. Stranded on the remote, blustery island of Lambholm in Camp 60, a cheerless collection of thirteen huts, the Italians missed home, sunshine, freedom and the opportunity to practise their Catholic faith in their own chapel.

The arrival of a new commandant, Major Buckland, changed things dramatically: he acquired two corrugated-iron Nissen huts, joined them together, then placed prisoner Domenico Chiocchetti in charge of designing and building a sanctuary at one end. While Major Buckland begged and borrowed the materials, Chiocchetti set to work with the help of a small band of fellow prisoners to create a masterpiece from plasterboard, scrap metal and sheer ingenuity.

The altar centrepiece is a painting of the Madonna and child, copied from a holy picture given to Chiocchetti by his mother, which he carried with him throughout the war. On either side he painted the glass of two arched windows with lovely images of St Francis of Assisi and St Catherine of Siena. The prisoners' welfare fund helped out with a pair of gold curtains needed for the back of the sanctuary, while the candelabra were moulded from stair treads of old blockships and the lanterns from bully-beef cans!

When the beauty and craftsmanship

of the finished sanctuary showed up the wretchedness of the rest of the Nissen hut, more plasterboard was found on which Chiocchetti painted a brickwork and carved stone interior, bringing unexpected Italian style to this corner of Camp 60. Finally the prisoners tackled the outside by adding an impressive façade and archway decorated by a thorn-crowned head of Christ made from red clay. A bell tower stands above, now housing a real bell, although a cardboard cutout was hurriedly inserted for the proud photograph of Chiocchetti and his fellow worker, Palumbo, taken in 1945 before they left for home.

Soon afterwards, when the order was given to flatten the camp, somehow the chapel remained,

LEFT:
Maria Chiocchetti,
widow of the chapel's
creator, one month
after his death

together with the statue of St George and the dragon which was another of Chiocchetti's masterpieces. In other words, everything that catered for the PoWs' material needs disappeared, but the two expressions of their spiritual needs still stand.

In the 1960s, Chiocchetti was tracked down to his home in Moena in the Dolomites, and returned to Camp 60 to spend three deeply moving weeks renovating his artwork. When he returned to Italy, he said he was leaving a part of his heart there.

That's how it feels when you visit the chapel today – as if faith poured out of a devoted heart and soul to create a little bit of heaven in the hell of wartime.

Just a month after Chiocchetti's death in May 1999, his widow, Maria, made an emotional visit to the Orkneys where she and her family were greeted with loving affection by the local people who look after the chapel. Nowadays, 75,000 visitors a year make their way to this faraway corner to see for themselves the

Nissen hut that was an inspiration in wartime, and is a memorial of craftsmanship and faith today.

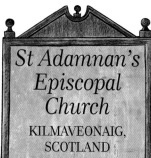

St Adamnan's Episcopal Church

KILMAVEONAIG, SCOTLAND

On the way from Pitlochry to beautiful Blair Castle on the Atholl estate, you could almost miss the turning that leads through a field of cows to the tiny, picturesque church of St Adamnan. There has probably been a church on this site for about 1,300 years, although the village of Kilmaveonaig, which was barely more than a few houses and a school, faded away in Victorian times when the building of a new road and the coming of the railway drew people away to Blair Atholl. They left behind a little church with a history of mixed fortunes, having faced damage, persecution, disrepair and rebuilding with great spirit and resolution.

Much of the damage came about as a result of the persecution of the Episcopal Church during the Reformation, when Presbyterianism became regarded as the established church in Scotland. Today, the Scottish Episcopal Church is a province of the worldwide Anglican Communion, but throughout the seventeenth and eighteenth centuries, especially during the time of the Penal Laws, which were repealed in 1792, Episcopalians in Scotland were not allowed to possess any churches or chapels, and it was illegal for clergy to minister to more than five people at a time. For the first offence, the penalty was six months' imprisonment. In fact, after Reverend Walter Stewart saw his church in Kilmaveonaig destroyed, he was charged, in 1756, with the dreadful offence of having performed divine service in his own house every Sunday for a year, with more than four people present in addition to his own family. At the age of seventy, he was convicted and committed to a particularly harsh prison at Perth Tolbooth for six months. Good job he was not convicted a second time, because the penalty would have been transportation to the American plantations as a slave for life!

Tales abound of the priest guarding his church overnight in the small upstairs chamber, complete with its simple bed, although in fact this room was a much later addition to the top

back corner of the church. It stands
to one side of the gallery from where
you can look down on the neat rows of
wooden seating below. The pews are of
very precise measurements, so we
learn from the architect's plans for
the restoration of the church in 1794,
which are displayed on the wall.
Eighteen inches per person were
allowed for the laird and his family,
while the common folk had to squeeze
themselves into seventeen inches
each! All in all, there were estimated
to be 258 seats in the church – rather
more than are needed for the small
congregation which now gathers there
on Sunday mornings. I wonder how
often they recall the old tradition that

parishioners could be buried inside the church under their favourite pew – not a very comforting thought!

The Robertsons of Lude have been great benefactors of St Adamnan's since 1591, and apart from having their own vault, names of their family

is a popular venue for weddings, with its pretty lich-gate looking much older than the century or so it actually is. It is the finishing touch to this little church with a long history of keeping the faith through challenge, neglect – and a great deal of love.

members adorn the walls, particularly on two huge funerary hatchments on the side walls – large decorated wooden plaques which traditionally hung on the castle door for up to a year after a death in the family.

It's little wonder that St Adamnan's

I love this cathedral – which may surprise those who've simply seen the exterior of the round, grey, spiked 1960s' structure which locals affectionately call 'Paddy's wigwam'! How can a building that looks so functional on the outside have the presence and dignity of a cathedral within?

I'll never forget the moment I had my first glimpse inside – the scale, shape, atmosphere and glorious colour which still take my breath away after so many visits. This huge inspiring cathedral manages to combine reverence and authority with a homeliness and intimacy that welcome the visitor, whether part of a 2,500-strong congregation, or simply seeking a quiet corner for a moment of private prayer.

There is a proud tradition of the Catholic faith in Liverpool, where many families can trace their history back to those who came across from Ireland after the potato famine in the mid-nineteenth century. By the turn of the nineteenth century, the desire for the city to have its own Catholic cathedral was well established, and in 1933, the foundation stone was laid for a grand brick and stone masterpiece designed by Sir Edwin Lutyens. War, combined with the huge expense and length of time needed for such a creation, halted work in the late 1950s, when only the crypt chapel had been completed. Today, that crypt is still used for worship, providing atmospheric surroundings in stark contrast to the style of the cathedral which later rose above it.

The aim was to spend no more than one million pounds on building

79

■ Roman Catholic
Metropolitan Cathedral
of Christ the King,
Liverpool

ABOVE AND OPPOSITE:
Two stations
of the cross

'a cathedral of our time'. In the end, Sir Frederick Gibberd, the architect who had earlier designed London Airport and Harlow New Town, won the commission, and the result is a practical plain building brought to life by stunning stained-glass windows which throw shafts of richly coloured light, creating different atmospheres in individual corners. The twelve chapels each have their own feel and beauty, from the warm carved and painted wood of St Joseph's Chapel, and the simplicity of the Lady Chapel, to the Children's Chapel which is perhaps the most poignant. Beside the sandstone statue of Christ surrounded by children, which was originally designed to be clambered over and explored by little hands and feet, a single candle has been lit in memory of 'all babies with no known resting place'. The memorial has been placed here by the Union of Catholic Mothers, to provide a place of prayer for those who grieve for stillborn or unborn babies lost through miscarriage or abortion, and children who have died soon after birth. The statue is constantly surrounded by fresh

wreaths and simple bunches of flowers, together with emotional loving cards naming babies who are still missed and remembered.

The altar is most striking for its simplicity, and its positioning in the centre of the huge circle of seats from which even those at the back can see clearly. Floating high above the sanctuary is the 2,000 ton lantern tower, a masterpiece of architecture and artistry which cascades light down onto the altar by day, and becomes a warm beacon for the darkened city at night.

Your eyes will be drawn to the huge

and intricate wall hangings with their bold inspiring messages which provide bright patches of colour on otherwise grey walls. These are all designed and made by Sister Anthony and her team of enthusiastic volunteers – and if you're really lucky, you might manage a peep inside her workroom above the crypt, which is an Aladdin's cave of half-finished tapestries and clerical robes, some for the cathedral, and others commissioned by churches far and wide.

For me, though, this cathedral is at its best when full of worshippers, as it has been on the occasions when I have

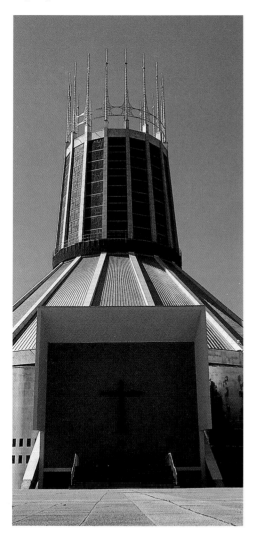

Sister Anthony and team in the workroom

presented live television programmes from there. One such broadcast was a moving service of tribute to Princess Diana the day after her funeral, in which the emotions and prayers of the congregation were enhanced by the empathy and presence of this great cathedral which is truly 'of our time'.

O K, I own up, I'm biased. As an official 'fair maid of Kent', having been born on the appropriate side of the River Medway, I have a built-in fondness for the county known as 'the garden of England'. In particular, the windswept triangle of marshland between Rye and Hythe, which has been created and added to by centuries of accumulated silt, has always held a fascination for me.

The coast of France is only a short sea crossing away from this exposed corner of England, and in centuries gone by, that simple fact brought great prosperity to the area from exports of the burgeoning wool trade. In those days, places which now are sleepy, out-of-the-way villages were bustling towns where successful merchants demonstrated both their affluence and their standing with God by building beautifully impressive churches.

Romney Marsh Churches
KENT

St Clement, Old Romney

T his is a perfect example of just such a church. In Elizabethan times, the original Cinque Port of Romney was a thriving town in the sheltered harbour of the bay. As the sea receded, the community declined, leaving the church of eleventh- or twelfth-century origins standing on a man-made mount to raise it above flood level.

Two surprises greet you as you open the church door. Firstly, it looks familiar, as indeed it would be to anyone who saw the 1960s' film *Dr Syn*, based on the famous book by Russell Thorndike. The church's complete set of eighteenth-century furnishings, which includes not just the pews, but also the pulpit, reading desk and minstrel gallery, was exactly what the Rank Organisation needed for the film – and in fact, that decision leads onto the second surprise inside St Clement. The box pews and all the rest of the woodwork are *pink*, painted rather as an

Gordon Finn-Kelcey, churchwarden of St Clement, Old Romney, for more than fifty years

■ ROMNEY MARSH
CHURCHES,
Kent

eighteenth-century house would have been. The colour was chosen by the Rank film producers, and the locals grew to like it so much that pink it has remained! But then, this is a community which likes continuity; in fact, in the past, at least two rectors and a churchwarden have each served the church for around half a century.

St Augustine, Brookland

One of the problems of building churches on a marsh is that they sink. Just take a look at St Augustine, and you'll see what I mean. Buttresses have been buffered up against the outside walls, and, inside, the arches that line the aisle all lean at a variety of jaunty angles. It's no surprise, then, that after two unsuccessful attempts to place a bell tower in the usual place at the top of the church, the congregation finally gave up. Instead, they came up with the solution of placing the six-bell tower, with its cedar shingle tiles, to one side of the church – and the result is one of the most picturesque sights of Kent. Inside St Augustine, climb into one of the magnificent box pews, and you soon realise that with wooden seating right round the inside edge of each box, almost half of the congregation are likely to be sitting with their backs to the vicar – not that he'd be able to see much of his flock anyway, as the boxes are so high. Apparently, children have always been given special dispensation to stand on the seats, so the minister knows if they are paying attention even if their parents are dozing quietly! Perhaps that's why they still talk in these parts of the verger who, around sixty years ago, was known for tickling the noses of snoozing congregation members with a horse's tail on the end of a short rod!

St Thomas, Fairfield

This is a special favourite of mine, the smallest church in Kent, a tiny building standing solitary on a broad stretch of rolling marshland. Drainage has always been a problem for the Marsh churches, and until the early 1960s St Thomas was often completely surrounded by water in the winter months. In fact, local people still speak today of paddling out to services and wedding ceremonies by rowing boat! In 1913, when much of the church was rebuilt, a raised causeway was constructed, and that's still the path you follow as you make your way to the door under the curious stare of the sheep who seem to think they have a lot more right to be there than you do!

Inside there are the same traditionally painted box pews, which would have been rented out, each with their own locking door. And cast an eye over the wonderful triple-decker pulpit, one of only three to be found in Kent. The altar is unusual,

too, in that it is completely enclosed. This is a relic of the old problem for remote country churches in years gone by, when dogs and other animals wandered in with no respect at all for the sanctity of the place! A fence around the altar usually did the trick – and it's a touching reminder today of the very down-to-earth challenges facing generations of worshippers in rural communities like that of St Thomas, Fairfield.

Mention Shrewsbury Abbey to most people nowadays, and one name will pop into their minds: Brother Cadfael. Our television screens have been filled in recent years with unforgettable tales of medieval detective work by the gentle yet worldly Benedictine monk who solves twelfth-century mysteries with intuitive skills which would be the envy of many a modern-day policeman. So intriguing are both the stories and Cadfael's character that visitors still occasionally arrive at Shrewsbury Abbey expecting to see rooms and halls that have become familiar through the television series, and asking to see where poor Cadfael is buried!

He's a figment of imagination, of course – the imagination of a delightful and prolific author whom I had the pleasure of meeting twice on my trips to Shrewsbury. Ellis Peters is the pen-name she chose when she wrote her Cadfael tales, but in fact Edith Pargeter was already known as the writer of dozens of books including historical novels and travel

Shrewsbury Abbey
(Abbey of St Peter and St Paul and Parish Church of the Holy Cross)
SHREWSBURY

guides. I find it hard even now, several years after her death in 1995, to walk into the abbey and not picture Edith during our recording of *Songs of Praise* a few years ago, sitting in the choir stalls not far from the magnificent altar front designed by John Pearson, and lovingly worked by the Ladies of Leek in the late 1880s.

Edith chose for her first Cadfael novel a tale which is part of the abbey's real history: the legend of St Winifred, who drew pilgrims from far and wide when rumours of miracles spread after her bones were brought to Shrewsbury in 1137. She had been a young seventh-century nun whose head was reportedly cut off by Prince Caradog when she rejected his advances. His dastardly deed led to a fitting end when the ground opened up and swallowed him, and a well of water sprang from the earth where her head had fallen. And to make the happy ending complete, Winifred's uncle, St Beuno, was able to reunite her head and body so that she could go on living for another fifteen years!

90

Her legend is told in a stained-glass window designed in 1992 by Jane Gray, who later created a window dedicated to the praise of St Benedict and the memory of Edith Pargeter, which includes Cadfael, a book and a range of herbs among its images.

The building is all the more welcoming because of the warm red glow of its old sandstone walls – but

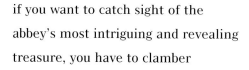

■ SHREWSBURY ABBEY
(ABBEY OF ST PETER
AND ST PAUL),
Shrewsbury

if you want to catch sight of the abbey's most intriguing and revealing treasure, you have to clamber

upstairs to the rooftop. There you'll find one of the oldest lead roofs in the country, enhanced by its graffiti! Since the 1700s, builders and craftsmen, bellringers and choirboys have used sharp tools to draw round their shoes, feet, hands and arms. One look at my size-six shoes compared with the little pointed slippers probably worn by a burly builder several centuries ago, and I realised how Gulliver must have felt!

ABOVE AND RIGHT:
Centuries of graffiti
on the lead roof

Many moons ago, when I had considerably more puff than I do now, I was a member of the Black and White Minstrel Show in Paignton, Devon. Most of the girls were dancers, but four of us were taken on primarily as singers. It was that quartet of 'Mitchell Maids' who, on Sunday mornings, often slipped away from the seaside town of Paignton to the quiet river-estuary setting of the village of Stoke Gabriel. There we sat at the back of St Mary's Church during the Eucharist service, soaking up the peace and presence of this gracious old church.

The memory of those visits comes back so clearly to me over the years. The building itself has changed little since I was there more than two decades ago, but then what would I expect of a church that has been a place of worship for seven centuries, and probably more? The church is dedicated to Mary, mother of Jesus, and the Archangel Gabriel, and although the tower dates back to the

St Mary and St Gabriel
STOKE GABRIEL, DEVON

thirteenth century, in the fifteenth century the body of the church was completely rebuilt in the classical perpendicular Gothic style of that period. Most spectacular of what remains from those long-gone medieval days is the rood-screen in exquisitely carved oak with painted-wood panels showing the New Testament saints with their halos, and the Old Testament prophets wearing their Tudor caps. Around the same age as the screen is the pulpit, also carved in oak in the wineglass style which is so typical in Devon. Much of its ancient colour is still to be seen, with fine detail of grapes and vines decorating the pulpit on all sides. The four evangelists, Matthew, Mark, Luke and John, look down on the altar from the reredos under the arched oak roof.

Lining the aisle are lovely Victorian brass lamps, still lit by oil, but only for one occasion in the year, the last Sunday of Advent, when they add a warm glow to the service of nine lessons and carols. One of the stained-glass windows is in memory

ABOVE:
The beautifully
decorated pulpit

of the Churchward family, the local squires for many years. The last in the line, Charlie Churchward, is still remembered affectionately for his feckless lavishness – such as the time he bartered a field for a bottle of whisky. And one vicar of St Mary's rates high on the list of Stoke Gabriel personalities. 'Parson' Nevill was a tall, handsome Irishman who

held the post around the 1900s. Story has it that all the local daughters fell in love with him, and that one even had a window specially made in her house on the other side of the river so that she could gaze at him! Sadly, all their hopes were dashed when he married his housekeeper who already had two children of her own.

Take a tip from me. Make time to sit on a bench in the graveyard, and treat yourself to one of the loveliest views in England, looking out over the mill creek and across the quayside towards the River Dart.

If you're lucky, as I was when I last visited, you'll hear the bells ringing – and Stoke Gabriel is extremely proud of its bell-ringing team which is one of the best in the county.

And if you want to remind

yourself about how fleeting our
time here is, go and sit under the
branches of the huge yew tree which
has spread its boughs across the
churchyard for 1,000 years. Like the
church itself, it stands firm and

unmoved as we play out our short,
frantic lives around it.

ABOVE:
A panel of the
rood-screen

When David Hope was just ten years old, he won a choral scholarship to the cathedral in Wakefield, the town where he lived. He was no stranger to the cathedral, as his cousin Muriel had started taking him there some years before. He grew to love the place – the smell of incense, the rich colour of the wooden pews and high vaulted ceiling; the glorious sound of the organ as music fills this church which is at once splendid and warmly welcoming. He especially loved Lent, when sackcloth was placed over the reredos at the back of the altar, to be removed on Easter Day in glorious celebration of the risen Christ. From his seat beyond the screen among the other boy sopranos in the choir stalls, he could look across to the throne where the Bishop sat, resplendent in his robes.

The images, sensations and inspiration of those childhood memories have stayed with him. Thirty-five years later, David sat in that same throne himself as the Bishop of Wakefield – and today, he

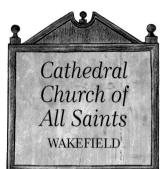

Cathedral
Church of
All Saints
WAKEFIELD

has influence over the lives and worship of thousands of Christians in his role as the Archbishop of York.

This cathedral has been described as a history book carved in stone, in which every generation of citizens in Wakefield has left its mark. The Saxons certainly worshipped on this site before William the Conqueror invaded. Over the centuries since then, walls, roofs and arches have been added, then removed and replaced in later years; towers have been built only to crumble again. What remains today is largely fifteenth century, with traces of stones and brickwork from earlier times. However, by the middle of the nineteenth century, the patching-up work of the previous 150 years was beginning to show in the perilous state of the building. Congregations were large following the Napoleonic wars and the prosperity of the Industrial Revolution, and a determined effort was made to create the church we now see. The tower was recased, and the spire taken down and rebuilt to its original height, making it the tallest in Yorkshire at nearly 250 feet. The crowning glory was the marvellous collection of windows by Charles Kempe, which he worked on over thirty-five years of his life. His familiar trade mark of a sheaf of corn can be found on all his windows in Wakefield Cathedral – and when you've spotted them, see if you can spy the mice hidden among the carving by Robert Thompson in St Mark's Chapel. I bet the search for those mice has kept many a choirboy amused during overlong sermons in the past!

I have three particular favourites here. Firstly, the golden figures designed by the twentieth-century architect William Comper, which stand

The Archbishop of York, Dr David Hope

■ CATHEDRAL CHURCH
OF ALL SAINTS,
Wakefield

on top of the rood-screen, are just stunning; they depict Jesus on the cross, Mary and John, and the angels from the book of Ezekiel. Secondly, the statue of Mary and child in the Lady Chapel is so lifelike and charming that people can't help patting it – hence its affectionate nickname, 'Madonna of

ABOVE:
'Madonna of the Dirty Knees'

the Dirty Knees'! Lastly, the warm colours and uniform neatness of the kneelers, which line every row of pews, tell of the many hours of patient stitching and love that have obviously gone into the making of them. They add a homeliness to this grand old church. No wonder David Hope loves it. To come here from the splendour of York Minster must truly feel to him like coming home.

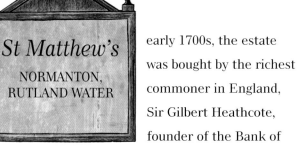

I magine an elegant church building which would have looked at home in London in the mid-nineteenth century; cut it horizontally across the middle so that only the top level and tower can be seen; set it afloat in calm shining water – then you can picture St Matthew's.

This church is visually stunning. I simply couldn't resist including it, even though in some ways it is now inappropriate for a book that celebrates Christian spirit, past and present. There is little doubt that there has been Christian worship on this spot for probably 1,000 years – and yet today, because of dramatic physical changes around it, St Matthew's is deconsecrated, and has been made into a museum by Anglian Water.

For centuries, this area of Normanton was home to a series of the richest families in the country, living in a manor house which grew in grandeur and opulence to match the wealth they gained mostly from sheep farming and trading. Eventually, in the early 1700s, the estate was bought by the richest commoner in England, Sir Gilbert Heathcote, founder of the Bank of England and Lord Mayor of London. By this time, the house had become a great Palladian mansion, and in order to expand their estate, the family began to pull down what had been the thriving village of Normanton, leaving the parish church of St Matthew's sadly isolated. What it became from then on was a much-loved family chapel and burial place, renovated in 1764 (as you can see from the foundation stone of that year which is still displayed on the wall) by rebuilding the nave and chancel, but leaving the original fourteenth-century tower as it was. By 1826, that old tower was quite unsafe, and the leading architects of the time, Thomas Cundy and his son, were called in to renovate St Matthew's. As surveyors to the Grosvenor Estates in London's Westminster, the Cundys decided to base their design on St John's Church in Smith Square – hence the rather incongruous,

delightfully unexpected grandeur of this country church at Normanton.

By the 1920s, the family's base had moved up north, and their home in Normanton was no longer needed. The great house was demolished, the estate broken up, and St Matthew's was left like a huge mausoleum, standing forlornly on a knoll in a field.

Then, in May 1970, the Empingham Reservoir Act was passed in Parliament, granting permission for the flooding of the area by diverting the River Gwash and constructing a dam wall. The construction work took three summers, and there were four more years of pumping before, in 1978,

Rutland Water became the largest reservoir in Europe.

The problem as the reservoir was being built was what to do with St Matthew's. In the end, a group of volunteers raised money to fill the crypt with rubble (carefully removing the remains of the affluent family members first!), then seal it with a layer of concrete, raising the ground level above the rising waters. What that created was a glorious church building which appears to float like a stately galleon on the glistening Rutland Water. Treat yourself to a visit – St Matthew's is a feast for the eyes.

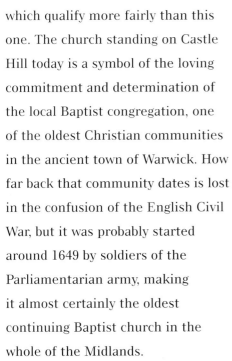

Castle Hill Baptist Church

WARWICK

When it comes to churches that are 'living and loved', it's hard to think of any which qualify more fairly than this one. The church standing on Castle Hill today is a symbol of the loving commitment and determination of the local Baptist congregation, one of the oldest Christian communities in the ancient town of Warwick. How far back that community dates is lost in the confusion of the English Civil War, but it was probably started around 1649 by soldiers of the Parliamentarian army, making it almost certainly the oldest continuing Baptist church in the whole of the Midlands.

All of which is a surprise as you stand at Eastgate, for centuries the main crossing point in the town, and look across at the splendid new honey-coloured building which opened its doors in spring 1999. In fact, you could be forgiven for thinking you are looking at several separate buildings, rather than the single integrated church you discover inside. That is because in Warwick, the older the building, the more comfortably it fits in with the style of the town, so any change is rightly viewed with reserve and caution. On one side of their Gothic Victorian church, which the Baptists hoped to demolish and replace when they started their planning in 1993, was the old Castle Arms pub, which the congregation had struggled to buy a few years earlier and was already using as an outreach café. On the other side stood a delightful row of almshouses. The local authority insisted that the style of both buildings should be reflected at either side of any new structure – and that has been achieved, by erecting a two-storey building where the pub lounge bar used to be, in the same semi-classical stuccoed style as the original pub, and by creating on the other side a new wing in red brick and tile which matches as nearly as possible the look and materials of the almshouses. In the middle, linking the stucco and brick, is a welcoming building, which reflects in modern style the pinnacles of Eastgate.

One fascinating discovery during the

demolition of the old Victorian church was a long glass cylinder found in the hollow foundation stone which turned out to be a 'time capsule'. Carefully stored inside were papers relating to the life and atmosphere of the church as the earlier congregation planned the erection of their new building in 1866. The local newspaper bearing the date of their Foundation Day, plus

the speech from the service, make wonderful reading. Also enclosed was an appeal letter, which proves that fundraising in churches is probably as established a practice as faith itself – and I especially loved the notice about the foundation ceremony which even gives the price of a cup of tea! Thankfully, some priorities never change!

Recognising their own delight in their unexpected find, the present-day congregation refilled the cylinder with similar documents relating to the day of their recent ceremony for the new building, and that cylinder is now snugly hidden in the old foundation stone, placed in the new church, perhaps to be discovered by a future community of Baptist worshippers.

What you find now on Castle Hill is a practical, modern church which reflects the history of its surroundings while reaching out to draw in today's generation – a church which is truly living, loved and relevant to our faith at the start of a new millennium.

ABOVE:
Hi-tech stage
management for
enthusiastic worship

Westminster Cathedral

LONDON

It was years ago that I first set foot in Westminster Cathedral, and was instantly hooked. There's something about this huge, impressive oasis of calm in the heart of bustling London that pleases the eye, lifts the soul and soothes the nerves.

Of course, it is a bit of a surprise to turn the corner from Victoria Street to find a Byzantine treasure that would be quite at home in Venice. You can imagine how the Victorians raised an eyebrow when, at the request of Cardinal Herbert Vaughan, architect John Bentley started building, in June 1895 on the site where a house of correction for paupers once stood. There was opposition to the cathedral from the highest quarters. It was derided as a monstrosity and labelled 'Vaughan's folly' – and sad to say, neither of these two men of vision ever saw their dream realised. Bentley died a year before the first major service took place in 1903, which was in fact the requiem for Cardinal Vaughan. At that point, the ornate decoration of the place had hardly begun, with the honey-coloured brickwork of the huge arched ceiling left bare. It's still bare today, and looks to me like the walls of a railway siding, but I like the thought that it's been blackened by a century of London grime, and the smoke from millions of candles lit by the faithful.

What I love most about Westminster Cathedral are its corners. This is a place to explore. Take a turn in any direction off the main area and you'll come across a treat: the glittering gold extravagance of the Chapel of St Gregory and St Augustine; the Chapel of St Patrick with its proud plaques of the Irish regiments who fought in the First World War; the Eric Gill carving above the altar in St George's Chapel, from which the monkey originally holding onto Sir Thomas More's right hand was removed when the cardinal of the day, Cardinal Griffin, objected to it. And don't miss the Lady Chapel, with its glorious glowing mosaic ceiling that depicts the life of Mary in breathtaking beauty.

Visit at any time of day, and you'll see solitary people quietly in prayer. Sometimes they cry. Occasionally, they sleep – and the sound of gentle snoring behind you is oddly reassuring in this majestic place which has the

■ WESTMINSTER
CATHEDRAL,
London

RIGHT:
'The sound of gentle
snoring is oddly
reassuring in this
majestic place which
has the feel of home'

feel of home. If you time it right, you may be lucky enough to hear the choir singing Vespers, which is immensely moving. In the past I was luckier still, and found a seat for a service taken by the late, and much-missed, Cardinal Hume himself. I have a delightful memory of coming across him chuckling like a schoolboy, as he waited in a side corridor with the choir and dignitaries all in full regalia, ready to process into a service we were televising. He was a wonderful man, at once inspirational and comfortingly down-to-earth – a bit like Westminster Cathedral itself!

Winchester
Cathedral
WINCHESTER

If those walls could only speak! So often in old churches I think that – but never more so than in the great Cathedral of Winchester, the 'capital of kings' like Canute and William Rufus, whose mortuary boxes balance precariously above your head as you walk down the aisles. The stories of history are told in the very fabric of this building. There is Joan of Arc's statue which glares towards the tomb of Cardinal Beaufort, the chancellor of England who played his part in her execution; the wall-paintings in the Holy Sepulchre Chapel depicting Christ's crucifixion which were lifted to reveal hidden below earlier paintings of Jesus in the tomb; the Holy Hole where pilgrims would lie on the floor with their hands reaching through as near as possible to the bones of St Swithin – remember him? Forty days of downpour if it rains on St Swithin's Day? And, wonder of wonders, the glorious thirteenth-century tiled floor not only survives today, but we're even allowed to walk on it! My favourite of all is the west window, which might stop you in your tracks when you first see it. In this giant mosaic nothing is quite where it should be, with half a face here, and a bit of foot there. History again! Back in the seventeenth century when Cromwell ruled England and the Puritan forces destroyed some of the most beautiful works of art in the cathedral, they smashed the west window. The slithers of glass were lovingly collected by local people who later tried to piece it back together – which they did, in a manner of speaking! Look at it now you know the story, and their dedication and determination bring a lump to the throat.

So many famous names are recalled here: Jane Austen, whose gravestone manages to omit any mention of her literary talent, and Isaak Walton who lies in the Chapel of St John and the Fishermen Apostles, a fitting resting place for the writer known as the 'father of angling'.

In fact, water flows through not just the story, but the foundations of

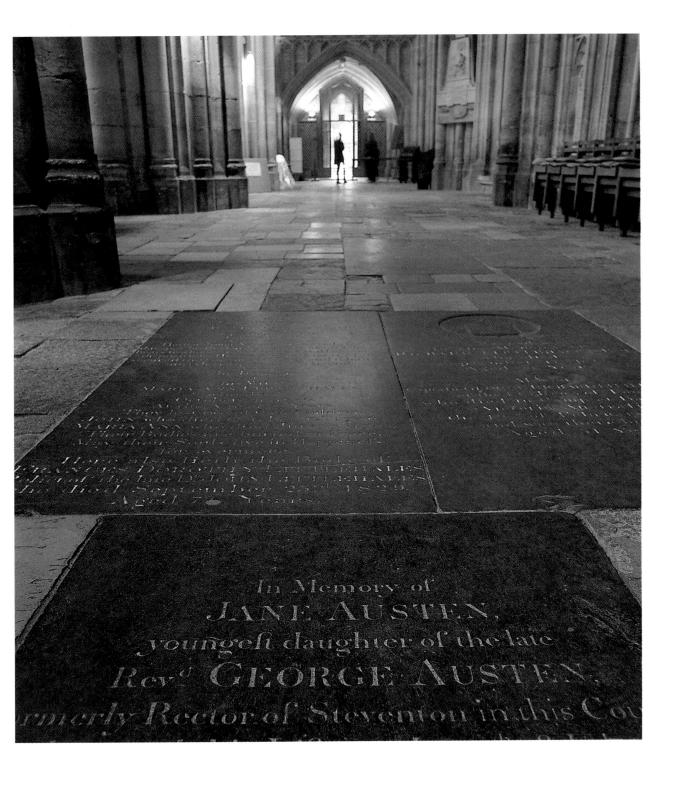

In Memory of
JANE AUSTEN,
youngest daughter of the late
Revᵈ GEORGE AUSTEN,
ormerly Rector of Steventon in this Cou

this cathedral which is built on waterlogged marshy ground. Take a look at the jaunty angle at which the arch at the end of the south aisle leans. In the early 1900s, the subsidence was so worrying that William Walker, a deep-sea diver, worked underwater for five years

ABOVE:
Statue of
Joan of Arc

RIGHT:
The Holy Hole,
surrounded
by icons,
marking the
original site
of St Swithin's
shrine

propping up the base of the outer walls with concrete cement. To get an idea of their problem, pack your wellies and visit the crypt in January – to see Antony Gormley's melancholy statue up to its knees in muddy water!

LEFT:
Wall-painting in the
Holy Sepulchre Chapel

BELOW:
Statue by Antony
Gormley in the crypt

I'll never forget the dreadful half-hour when I thought *Songs of Praise* had set fire to Windsor Castle! In November 1992, news reached us all that the chapel at Windsor was ablaze, probably as a result of an electrical fire. Knowing that our scaffolders and electricians were in St George's Chapel that day, setting up for the Advent *Songs of Praise* we were due to record a few days later, there seemed no other explanation except that we had done it! When I finally learned that the fire was in a smaller chapel my relief was immense, not least because the thought

of damage to the glorious chapel of St George would be a sadness not just for Britain, but for the many thousands of visitors who make their way there every year from all over the world.

It's a measure of the spirit of the people who live and work at the castle that, despite the devastation, they insisted we should carry on with making our programme. But perhaps that's no surprise when you recall that the chapel is the spiritual centre of the Order of the Garter, the oldest existing monarchical order of chivalry, founded by the 'warrior king' Edward III in about 1347 with King Arthur and the Knights of the Round Table in mind. The Military Knights, the Knights' Companions and the Royal and Foreign Knights, who are all members of the Order today, are part of a long and proud tradition. So, too, is the community of priests and laymen at the College of St George, which was also established in about 1347 for the spiritual support of the Order. The Military Knights, all distinguished soldiers who have now retired, live

Major Jim Cowley,
OBE, DCM, *aged*
eighty, outside
St George's Chapel

*The ancient castle and
chapel of Windsor need
modern-day security*

within the walls of the castle so that they can fulfil their duty to represent the Knights of the Garter at worship in St George's Chapel. If you are able to go along to a Sunday morning service, you may see the Military Knights taking part, and there are few sights more splendid than my friend, Major Jim Cowley, in scarlet uniform. Perhaps it is particularly moving for me, as my uncle, Arthur (Jack) Wollaston, was a Military Knight until his death in 1991.

The chapel itself, with its large

perpendicular late Gothic windows and slender pillars, is light, delicate and elegant. It was created by a succession of monarchs, notably Henry VIII, who completed the fan vaulting over the crossing. It was Henry who had the carved wooden oriel window put into the private Edward IV chantry chapel above the altar, so that Catherine of Aragon could view the Garter Ceremony which men only could attend. This was the same window where Queen Victoria sat to take part in Sunday morning services. Many monarchs are buried or remembered here, including Henry VIII himself – and there are lifelike carvings on the tombs of Edward VII and Queen Alexandria, King George V and Queen Mary, plus those of countless other nobles and clerics. I found myself giving a nod of thanks towards the bust of Bishop Giles Thomson in the Bray Chantry (now the bookshop), who was one of the scholars responsible for the King James Version of the Bible published in 1611.

Of the many treasures and visual treats within the chapel, I especially like the individual style and dignity of the smaller chantry chapels, in which early morning communion is said in rotation. The magnificently designed organ case takes the eye through to the quire and chancel, resplendent with carvings by William Berkeley and Henry Emlyn. The Queen's Stall is

simply beautiful – and note the display along the wall of stall plates, helmets, banners and swords of the Garter Knights. With its unbroken tradition of choral worship spanning 650 years, St George's is famous for its choir school, and you can often see the robed choristers making their way through the cloisters on their way to chapel.

This is a glorious old building with a thousand stories to tell of monarchs and history-makers who have shaped the life we now enjoy. Centuries of worship and love are carved, etched and nurtured in this house of prayer which keeps tradition alive for us today.

The first time I saw this church, I was dangling on a cord twenty feet beneath an RAF

rescue helicopter! Daft what you get up to when you're a television presenter – but the winchman peering down at me was my interviewee on our *Songs of Praise* programme from the Isle of Anglesey, that fascinating corner of Wales where seventy per cent of the people speak in their own beautiful native language. Far beneath my boots, I glimpsed an ancient church standing in a field just a mile

or so away from the RAF base at Valley. On terra firma, while jet planes and helicopters whirr above your head, you step back in time the moment you climb over the stile and open the gate into the graveyard surrounding the tiny parish church of St Mary.

There was probably a church here as far back as the twelfth century, although the ancient parts which now remain are more likely to be relative youngsters from a couple of centuries later. Although much of the original fabric of the building has been kept, renovators nearly a century and a half ago replaced most of the roof timbers and slates, inserted new windows (although the lovely stained-glass medieval windows in the east wall were left untouched) and replaced the former box pews with open seating. Much of the cost of this work was underwritten by the railway company, whose line runs close to St Mary's on its way to Holyhead, the main crossing point to Ireland for both visitors and freight. Interestingly enough, you can tell from the church

registers how the coming of the railway made quite an impact on the rural community around St Mary's, which had been admirably self-sufficient, with shoe- and clog-makers, saddlers, millers, blacksmiths, weavers and bone-setters among its members. With the railway came new jobs for the congregation such as coal porter, fireman, signalman and engineer.

Churchgoing was a way of life then, with several services each Sunday for both Church in Wales congregations, and their nonconformist neighbours. In fact, going to church could be good fun, especially at St Mary's where, throughout the nineteenth century, young men entertained themselves with churchyard games such as weightlifting the heavy 'carreg gorchest', or contest stone (a pastime which only stopped when an older and wiser church official hid the stone before anyone injured themselves!), jumping competitions, and a form of tennis which involved throwing a ball onto the roof, then knocking it back up again before it hit the ground. That probably disturbed the birds who've enjoyed years of nesting in the tiny

bell tower – until recently the hole was blocked up to stop the evidence of their presence dropping onto the unsuspecting congregation below!

The twelfth-century font, in which hundreds of babies were baptised over the years, has long been moved for safe keeping to a church in Holyhead. Nowadays the altar is just a basic

wooden tea table, and the harmonium can't manage more than a squeak! Even the grand old wooden chest which used to hold the silver now provides a home for the Brasso and

■ St Mary's Church,
Llanfair yn Neubwll,
Valley, Anglesey, Wales

'Generations of
families are laid to
rest in the graveyard'

rubber gloves! But the faint feel of former glory at St Mary's belies the tremendous affection in which this little church is held. Generations of families are laid to rest in the graveyard, which only a few days before my last visit had seen the burial of Tom Pierce, who had probably done more than anyone to galvanise support for this local treasure.

They still speak nostalgically of harvest festivals in which farm folk carrying their own produce made their way along the well-worn tracks which lead to St Mary's. And every year, there is standing-room only at the annual service on the feast of St Mary in this little church, which is now seldom used, but dearly loved.

Holy Saviour Church

HITCHIN, HERTFORDSHIRE

For me, the most important church comes at the end of this book because it is here that I am a member of the congregation. Tucked away in the backstreets around Hitchin railway station, Holy Saviour Church is hardly in the most picturesque of areas. Many people in Hitchin may not even realise it is there! But this is our church in the middle of my own community, and it is the place of worship in which I feel most at home.

In 1863, when plans for a new church were first suggested by George Gainsford – a young curate at the nearby parish church of St Mary, who was wealthy enough to be able to put up the money himself – the area around Hitchin station was developing fast. New housing was needed for railway workers, tradesmen and farm labourers, and the green fields around the Walsworth Road area disappeared under rows of terraced houses. Today, when you discover Holy Saviour tucked away among roads of Victorian terraces, it's easy to overlook the pedigree of the building, which was designed by William Butterfield, a well-known architect of the time, who also had Keble College in Oxford to his credit. His design style, using red and blue brick and Bath stone, is very distinctive, and adds a warmth to the building both inside and out.

In fact, to step inside Holy Saviour is a delightful surprise. The patterned brick interior is colourful and welcoming, creating an intimacy which draws in the congregation as they worship together along the dark wooden pews. There is a formality here too, perhaps because of the high-church tradition Holy Saviour has followed since the earliest years when George Gainsford was vicar, and a robed choir, incense and colourful vestments are still a regular part of our services.

Being at the heart of what has become a multicultural and multi-faith community, Holy Saviour stands comfortably alongside its Sikh neighbours whose temple is now established in our old church hall. For years, the church building itself has also been used regularly for services by two black Christian churches. Our new hall is packed with community activities throughout the week, from mother and toddler groups, scout and brownie groups, to pensioners' get-togethers and social clubs. There's the Mothers' Union as well as prayer groups, confirmation classes, charity initiatives and fundraising, and a busy programme of working and worshipping with other churches of all denominations around Hitchin.

My neighbours and fellow Christians

But in that, Holy Saviour is typical of thousands of churches up and down the country. You may walk past your local church every day without realising how much energy, commitment and practical care comes from the congregation as they reach out into the community in an expression of their Christian faith. Their church is alive and vibrant – and it is God's love which they carry with them in their outreach to others.

If the church is God's house, then Britain has more than its share of exquisitely beautiful houses of worship which are built to his glory. But God doesn't confine himself to church buildings. His real home is the human heart. And because of that, however humble the architecture of the building or the area in which it stands, it is the people who are the church, and God who is truly LIVING AND LOVED.